POLAND

LETTERS FROM AROUND THE WORLD

Teresa Fisher

Photographs by Howard Davies

CHERRYTREE BOOKS

LETTERS FROM AROUND THE WORLD

Titles in this series

**AUSTRALIA • BANGLADESH • BRAZIL • CANADA • CHINA • COSTA RICA
EGYPT • FRANCE • GERMANY • GREECE • INDIA • INDONESIA
IRELAND • ITALY • JAMAICA • JAPAN • KENYA • MEXICO • NIGERIA
PAKISTAN • POLAND • RUSSIA • SAUDI ARABIA • SOUTH AFRICA
SPAIN • SWEDEN • THE USA**

A Cherrytree Book

Conceived and produced by

Nutshell
MEDIA

www.nutshellmedialtd.co.uk

VISIT OUR WEBSITE
Evans
www.evansbooks.co.uk

First published in 2009 by
Evans Brothers Ltd
2A Portman Mansions
Chiltern Street
London W1U 6NR

© Copyright Evans Brothers 2009

Editor: Cath Senker
Designer: Tim Mayer
Map artwork: Encompass Graphics Ltd
All other artwork: Tim Mayer

All photographs were taken by Howard Davies, apart
from page 13, which is courtesy of the Siekański family.

Acknowledgements
The photographer would like to thank the following for
all their help: Julia, Kasia, Krzysztof, Gosia and Andrzej
Siekański, Gabriela Toch, Błażej Dolicki, Julia Dukat,
Krzysztof Kwiatkowski, Jolanta Pierzchała and the staff
and pupils of Zespółu Szkół Społecznych, St John the
Baptist Catholic Church, Antoni Adamek cake shop,
Bożena Trylska and Barry and Anna Lee-Potter for their
support with the book and their hospitality in Kraków.

British Library Cataloguing in Publication Data
Fisher, Teresa
   Poland. – (Letters from around the world)
   1. Poland – Social life and customs – 21st century –
   Juvenile literature
   2. Poland – Social conditions – 21st century –
   Juvenile literature
   3. Poland – Geography – Juvenile literature
   I. Title
943.8'057

ISBN-13: 9781842345481

Cover: Julia and some of her classmates in the
playground at school.
Title page: Julia's teacher, Mrs Pierzchała, teaches the
class a song and a dance in their classroom.
This page: Farming is important in Poland. More than
half of the land is farmed.
Contents page: Julia (in the middle) with her two best
friends from school, Gaba and Julia.
Glossary page: A street performer, dressed as a statue,
entertains shoppers in the city centre in Kraków.
Further information page: This local cheese is made from
sheep's milk and comes in different shapes and sizes.
Index: Tourists visit the mountains in summer as well as
during the snowy winter months.

Contents

My Country

Thursday, 3 January

8 Wawel Castle Street
Prądnik Czerwony
Kraków 31–444
Poland

Dear Jo,

Cześć! (You say 'CH-ay-esch'. This means 'hello' in Polish.)

My name's Julia (you say 'YOO-lia') and I'm 9 years old. I live in a suburb of Kraków (KRAK-ov), a large town in southern Poland. I have a sister, Kasia (KA-sha), who's 14, and a brother, Krzysztof (K'SHISH-toff), who's 16.

Thanks for being my penpal. It will help me with my English.

Write back soon!

From

Julia

This is my family in our garden. I'm the one in the middle.

Poland is a large country in central Europe. In 2004, Poland joined the European Union. Now many Polish people live and work abroad.

Poland's place in the world.

Poland has borders with seven other countries. It takes 12–15 hours to drive from the mountains near Slovakia to the Baltic Sea in the north.

Most people in Poland live in large towns and cities, by the coast or on a river. Kraków is on the River Vistula, Poland's longest river.

More than 1 million people live in Kraków. It has many historic buildings, such as this church.

Kraków is one of the largest and oldest cities in Poland. It is more than 1,000 years old. It has a fine palace and many beautiful churches.

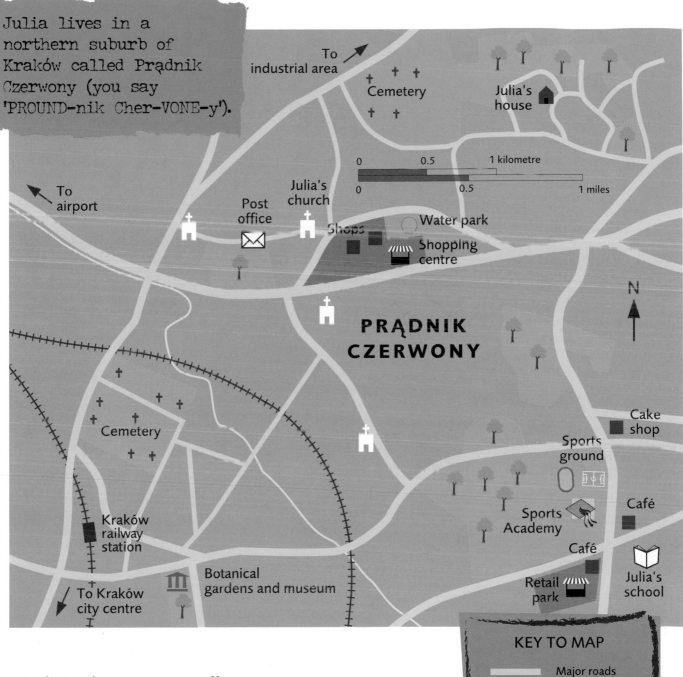

Julia lives in a northern suburb of Kraków called Prądnik Czerwony (you say 'PROUND-nik Cher-VONE-y').

To industrial area

Cemetery

Julia's house

To airport

0   0.5   1 kilometre
0   0.5   1 miles

Julia's church

Post office

Shops

Water park

Shopping centre

N

PRĄDNIK CZERWONY

Cemetery

Cake shop

Sports ground

Sports Academy

Café

Café

Kraków railway station

Botanical gardens and museum

Retail park

Julia's school

To Kraków city centre

Kraków has many colleges, museums and theatres as well as cafés, bars and restaurants. Nearby, there are three towns with lots of industries, and an airport. Kraków also has good railway links to other cities and neighbouring countries.

KEY TO MAP

Major roads

Railway

River

Churches

Parks

Built-up area

7

Landscape and Weather

The countryside near Kraków is a mixture of fields, hills and mountains. In the north of Poland, the land is flat with many lakes and forests. In the mountains there are animals such as wolves, wild cats and bears. On the coast, there are beautiful sandy beaches.

The River Vistula is more than 1,000 km long. It is linked to other rivers in eastern Europe and is important for transporting goods.

Summer in Poland is warm and sunny, although there is also plenty of rain. The winters are cold and snowy, particularly in the mountains.

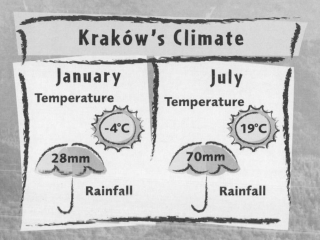

Kraków's Climate

January	July
Temperature	**Temperature**
-4°C	19°C
28mm	70mm
Rainfall	Rainfall

The Tatra Mountains, along the border with Slovakia, are especially cold in winter because of their height.

At Home

Julia lives in a modern terraced house, like many people in Prądnik Czerwony. It takes about 15 minutes to drive from her house in the suburb to the centre of Kraków by car.

Julia made this small flower garden in front of the house with her grandma. She now looks after it herself.

Julia's family like to play chess, a popular game in Poland. Here, Julia watches and learns from her brother and sister.

Julia's family have lived in the house for 11 years. It has a large living room, dining room, study, kitchen and bathroom. Julia and her brother and sister each have their own bedroom.

Julia has been learning to play the piano for three years. Her favourite composer is Frédéric Chopin, who was Polish.

Like most houses in Poland, Julia's house has central heating to keep it warm in the cold winters. The windows have double glazing to keep in the heat.

Julia likes to keep her bedroom neat and tidy. She does her homework in her room.

The family have a TV at home. Like many other Polish families, they also have a computer. Sometimes Julia uses the Internet to do her homework, but she prefers reading or playing with her toys.

During the summer, Julia and her sister Kasia spend time playing together in the back garden.

Friday, 28 January

8 Wawel Castle Street
Prądnik Czerwony
Kraków 31-444
Poland

Cześć Jo!

Did I tell you that we have a holiday home in Zakopane (you say 'zako-PAH-ne'), near the Tatra Mountains? It takes about two hours to drive there from Kraków. We often have holidays there, especially in the winter.

We love going to Zakopane. In the summer we go walking in the mountains. In the winter we ski and walk in the snow.

Do widzenia (This means 'goodbye'. You say 'DO-vit-zenia'.)

From

Julia

Here I am in Zakopane. I love playing in the snow.

Food and Mealtimes

In Poland, people eat four meals a day. On school days, Julia's family have breakfast together at around 7.20 a.m. Julia has a second breakfast at school just before 10 a.m. She usually drinks tea, but she prefers hot chocolate in winter.

For breakfast, Julia has bread, butter, cheese, cold meats, boiled eggs and fruit.

Julia has her second breakfast at school, sitting at her desk in the classroom.

Julia's family eat their main meal together. This meal is called *obiad* (you say 'OB-yad').

The main meal is after school, at about 3 p.m. There is usually soup, often made with beetroot or tomato, followed by a meat or fish dish. The family have fruit or cakes for dessert. The last meal of the day is between 7 and 8 p.m. It is a light supper, such as scrambled eggs, or toasted sandwiches with meat or cheese.

Most Polish people buy their food in little local shops and their fresh fruit and vegetables at local markets. In the larger towns and cities, many families do their weekly shopping at big supermarkets.

Cakes are a popular treat in Poland. The word for cake shop is *cukiernia* (you say 'tsu-KIER-nia'). It means 'made from sugar'.

In Kraków market, stallholders cook the popular 'hunters' stew', made with pork and cabbage, and served with fried potatoes.

Saturday, 2 March

8 Wawel Castle Street
Prądnik Czerwony
Kraków 31–444
Poland

Cześć Jo!

Here's a Polish recipe. It's for my favourite dish: *pierogi* (you say pier-OG-ee) – dumplings.

You need: 500g flour, 1 egg, 1 tablespoon of oil,
1 glass of warm water.

1. Mix all the ingredients into a dough.

2. Roll out the dough with a rolling pin. Cut it into flat, circular shapes using an upside-down cup.

3. Add the filling. My favourite is mashed potato with cheese and onion, or mincemeat. Fruit with sugar is also good.

4. Fold over the dough to make a half circle. Press down the edges carefully.

5. Ask an adult to cook the *pierogi* in boiling water for 5 minutes.

They're delicious served piping hot!

From

Julia

Here are my *pierogi*, which I made with my grandma.

School Day

Julia goes to a local primary school three kilometres from her home. Kasia and Krzysztof go the secondary school next door. Their mother takes them in the car. Most Polish children walk to school or catch the bus.

Julia's mother collects her from school. Like other Polish schoolchildren, Julia does not have to wear a school uniform.

Julia's class teacher, Mrs Pierzchała (you say 'Pierch-HOW-a') helps Julia and Gaba in the Polish language lesson.

In Poland, children start school at the age of seven.
At 13, they move to secondary school. They go to high
school at 16 for two to four years. There are two terms,
from September to February
and from March until mid-June.

Julia enjoys studying
music, drama and art
at school. Some of her
paintings are on the wall.

The school day starts at 8 a.m. and finishes at 2.30 p.m.
There is a mid-morning and an afternoon break.

Julia works on the computer with Gaba. Most Polish schools have computers.

Julia enjoys skipping in the playground with her friends during mid-morning break.

Every day the class studies Polish, mathematics, geography, history and science. Polish children learn at least one other language at school. Julia learns English and French. German is a popular language to learn too. Julia's favourite subject is drawing.

Julia studies hard. She has homework most days.

Monday, 27 April

8 Wawel Castle Street
Prądnik Czerwony
Kraków 31–444
Poland

Cześć Jo!

I'm glad you liked the *pierogi*.

Did I tell you that our school project this term is making a garden? We're learning about protecting the environment. We planted flowers this week, and I am in charge of watering them. When I was little, my grandma gave me the job of watering the flowers at home, so I'm good at caring for plants.

Do you learn about the environment at school?

Do widzenia

Julia

Each class has its own plot in the school grounds. We'll see whose plants do best!

Off to Work

Julia's dad works for the national telephone company. Her mum works at Kraków's Sports Academy (a university college for teaching PE), where she teaches sports psychology. It is normal in Poland for both parents to have a job.

Julia's mum talks to a student at the Sports Academy.

There are lots of different types of work in Poland, including shipbuilding, mining and farming. The main crops are potatoes, fruit, and leafy vegetables.

This farmer is making round haystacks. About one-sixth of working people in Poland farm the land.

Poland is rich in natural resources, such as gas and silver. It is Europe's largest producer of coal. Trees from the forests are used to make timber and paper.

Shipbuilding is an important industry on the northern coast, especially in Gdańsk.

SOŁDEK

Free Time

Julia spends her free time drawing, reading and playing in the garden with Krzysztof and Kasia. As a special treat, the family go to the water park near their house, to play on the waterslides.

Many Poles enjoy going to the theatre and cinema, playing football and going swimming.

This viewpoint near Kraków, called Kościuszko Mound (you say 'Kosh-TSCH-us-ko'), is a popular place to visit at the weekend.

Many school groups go on summer trips to the Tatra Mountains to learn about the environment.

Wednesday, 25 May

8 Wawel Castle
Street
Prądnik Czerwony
Kraków 31–444

Cześć Jo!

Guess what! Tomorrow is Mother's Day. While mum's out of the house I'm secretly making a present to show her how much I love her.

On Mother's Day in Poland, we like to draw pictures or make presents for our mums. At school we hold a special ceremony. How do people celebrate Mother's Day where you live?

I can't wait for your next letter!

Julia

I'm making mum a collage of a giraffe with coloured paper because it's her favourite animal. She's going to love it!

Religion and Festivals

Like most Polish people, Julia and her family are Roman Catholic. They go to Mass at their local church every Sunday.

Religious festivals are important in Poland. On 1 November it is All Saints Day. People visit the graves of their relatives to remember them. They decorate the gravestones with candles and flowers.

Julia and her family visit the grave of Julia's great-grandmother and light a candle in her memory.

At Christmas time, people decorate their houses with traditional Nativity scenes that look like churches.

Christmas and Easter are the biggest Roman Catholic festivals. At Christmas, most Polish people fast (go without food) for 24 hours before nightfall on Christmas Eve. They end their fast with a delicious feast, but with no meat.

There are many local festivals in Poland. For the Kraków Dragon Parade, each school makes its own dragon costume and joins a grand procession.

27

Fact File

Capital city: Warsaw. It has many old buildings, and important museums and art galleries. The president lives in a large palace.

Other major cities: Kraków, Gdańsk, Poznań, Szczecin and Wrocław.

Size: 312,679 km^2

Population: 38,500,696. Polish people are called Poles.

Language: Polish is the main language, spoken by 98% of the people. The Polish alphabet has 32 letters.

Main religion: About 90% of Poles are Roman Catholic. There are also small numbers of Eastern Orthodox, Protestants and other religious groups.

Flag: Poland's national flag has two colours. It is white on top and red on the bottom. White is for peace. Red is for the Polish people who have died in wars.

Main festivals: Christmas, New Year, Easter, Labour Day (1 May), All Saints Day (1 November).

Longest river: Vistula (1,047km).

Highest mountain: Mt Rysy (you say 'RY-sy'), 2,499m.

Currency: The zloty (you say 'ZWOT-ey'). There are 100 groszy (you say 'GRO-schy') in a zloty. Poland will soon start to use the euro, which is the currency used by most of the member countries of the European Union.

Famous people: Frédéric Chopin (1810–49) was a famous classical music composer, who loved writing piano music. Marie Curie (1867–1934) was an important chemist. Pope John Paul II (1920–2005) was the first Polish leader of the Roman Catholic Church. He came from a small Polish village near Kraków. Roman Polanski (born 1933) is one of the world's greatest film directors.

Main industries: Machine building, iron and steel, coal mining, chemicals, shipbuilding, food processing, glass, drinks and textiles.

Sport: Football is the most popular sport. A really keen football fan is called a *kibic* (you say 'Ki-BITZ'). Lots of people enjoy playing chess too.

Stamps: Polish stamps sometimes show popular festivals, sports and animals.

Glossary

climate The normal weather in a place.

composer A person who writes music.

Cześć! This means 'hello' in Polish.

double glazing Windows with two layers of glass to keep in the heat.

Do widzenia This means 'goodbye' in Polish.

European Union A group of 27 countries in Europe that work and trade together.

haystack A large pile of hay, left in a field to dry.

Mass A Roman Catholic ceremony to remember the last meal Jesus Christ had with his followers.

mining Digging minerals such as coal or silver out of the ground.

Nativity The birth of Jesus Christ.

natural resources Things in nature that can be used by a country, such as oil, coal and water.

parade A procession of people, often in costume.

pierogi Small, boiled dumplings that are filled with sweet or savoury fillings.

Pole The word for a Polish person.

psychology The study of the mind and how the mind works.

Roman Catholic A member of the Roman Catholic Church, the largest branch of Christianity. The head of this Church is the Pope.

saint A person who the Church sees as holy because of the way he or she lived or died.

suburb A small district at the edge of a town or city.

terraced house A house joined to other houses to form a row.

timber Pieces of wood, ready for building.

traditional Done in a way that has not changed for a very long time.

Further Information

Information books:

Countries of the World: Poland by J. Nichols (Evans Brothers Ltd, 2005)

Looking at Countries: Poland by Katie Dicker (Franklin Watts, 2009)

New EU Countries and Citizens: Poland by J. Kadziolka (Cherrytree Books, 2005)

A Visit to Poland by Vic Parker (Heinemann, 2008)

Welcome to Poland by Umaima Mulla-Feroze, Paul Grajnert and Dorothy L. Gibbs (Franklin Watts, 2005)

Fiction:

The Dragon of Krakow and Other Polish Stories by Richard Monte (Frances Lincoln, 2008)

Websites:

CIA World Factbook
https://www.cia.gov/library/
publications/the-world-
factbook/geos/pl.html
Key facts about the Polish people, geography, economy and government.

KidsKonnect – Poland
http://www.kidskonnect.com/content
/view/329/27/
A site with links to many websites about Poland.

Polish government website
http://www.poland.gov.pl
The official website, with pages about life in Poland and what to do and see there.

Polish National Tourist Office
http://www.poland.travel/en-gb/
Information about travelling to Poland.

Polish Recipes
http://www.magma.ca/~pfeiffer/
sharon/polish.htm.
Recipes for Polish soups, salads, main dishes and deserts.

Index